POSTER COLLECTION

RALPH SCHRAIVOGEL

09

Mit einem Essay von / Essay by Robert Massin

MUSEUM FÜR GESTALTUNG ZÜRICH
PLAKATSAMMLUNG/POSTER COLLECTION

LARS MÜLLER PUBLISHERS

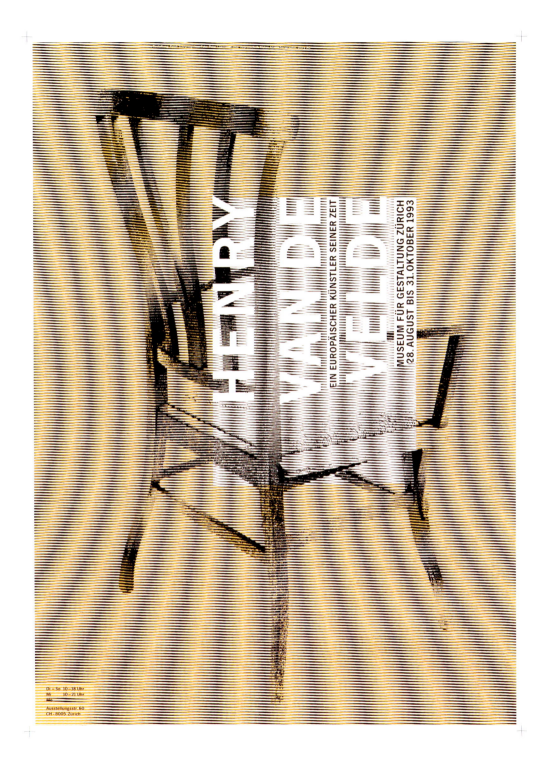

1 **Henry van de Velde / Museum für Gestaltung Zürich**
1993

VORWORT

Unter den vielen Kulturplakaten, die uns gleichgültig lassen, gibt es auch solche, die durch die geistreiche Behandlung des Themas oder die grafische Innovation bestechen. Und es gibt solche, die den Blick fesseln, vielleicht auch verstören, weil sie über ihre hohe grafische Qualität hinaus ein Ausmass künstlerischer Anteilnahme und Interpretation zeigen, das man von diesem Medium in der Regel nicht erwartet. In seiner nun zwanzigjährigen Tätigkeit als Plakatgestalter hat Ralph Schraivogel Arbeiten vorgelegt, von denen man ungewöhnlich viele zur letzten Kategorie zählen kann. Durch seine eigenwilligen Plakate ist Schraivogel in der Schweiz zu einer Figur «hors concours» geworden und zu einem Vorreiter einer neuen Generation von Gestaltern. An nationalen und internationalen Wettbewerben gewinnt er regelmässig höchste Anerkennung. Die Folge ist, dass man von ihm spricht wie von einem Mythos. Doch Mythen entstehen, wenn jemand Geheimnisse angedichtet werden, die er nicht hat: viel zu lange war die Rezeption von Schraivogel in der Faszination darüber gefangen, dass er in einer Art alchimistischer, letztlich unzeitgemässen Methode, so die Annahme, zu seinen Ergebnissen finde. Nachdem Ralph Schraivogel seit rund drei Jahren auch den Computer für seine Arbeiten beizieht, lässt sich nun noch besser zeigen, dass die technischen Hilfsmittel nebensächlich sind, das Entscheidende und Wegweisende dagegen sein heuristischer Arbeitsprozess. Man wird an vielen seiner Plakate etwas Kostbares feststellen können, das nicht einfach auf ihre eigenwillige Entstehungsweise oder den ausgeklügelten Druck zurückzuführen ist. Seine Plakate sind Ergebnisse von Arbeitsprozessen, die einen zeitlichen Spielraum einfordern, der weit über das Übliche hinausgeht. In seinem Atelier wollen Form und Inhalt nur dann gemeinsam zur vollen Reife kommen, wenn ihnen die dafür notwendige Zeit eingeräumt wird. Mit solchen Befreiungsschlägen zu Gunsten umsichtig gelenkter visueller Forschungsreisen nimmt Schraivogel freilich ein Privileg für sich in Anspruch, das einen gewissen Zwiespalt hinterlässt. Denn die Frage der Verhältnismässigkeit zwischen Auftrag und Ergebnis wird hier vom Designer selbst beantwortet. Doch vielleicht es ist genau das, was uns seine Plakate so kostbar macht. Er ist ein Grafiker, der sich mit Leib und Seele dem Plakat widmet und so dem latent anachronistischen Medium neue Impulse und eine neue Berechtigung verschafft. Legen wir ihn also auf einen neuen Auftrag fest (aber nicht zu gnädig) und geben wir ihm etwas Zeit (aber nicht zu grosszügig) – auf dass das viele noch mehr verspricht!

Felix Studinka

FOREWORD

A lot of cultural posters leave us completely cold, but others appeal because the theme is treated so wittily or the graphic design is so innovative. And then some capture our attention, or perhaps even distress us, because apart from their high graphic quality they show a degree of artistic sympathy and interpretation that we do not normally expect from this medium. Ralph Schraivogel has been working as a poster designer for twenty years now, and has produced an unusually large number of works that fall into the latter category. His highly individual approach has made Schraivogel into a figure who is "hors concours" in Switzerland, a pioneer for a whole generation of designers. He regularly wins top awards in national and international competitions. The consequence is that he is discussed as though he has almost mythical qualities. But myths arise because qualities that a person does not have are imputed to him: people's response to Schraivogel was dominated for far too long by fascination with the fact that he achieved his results through a kind of alchemy, ultimately using methods that were not appropriate to his time, or so the assumption ran. Ralph Schraivogel has been using a computer in his work for about three years now, and so it is easier to show that the technical aids are beside the point, that the key and ground-breaking factor is his heuristic working process. Many of his posters create a sense of high value that does not simply derive from their individual genesis or ingenious printing techniques. His posters are the result of working processes that demand a much greater than normal time input. In his studio, form and content can only mature fully and mutually if the necessary time is allotted to them. Striking such liberating blows for prudently guided visual exploration voyages admittedly means that Schraivogel is claiming a privilege for himself that generates a certain conflict. This is because in this case the question about relative qualities of commission and result is answered by the designer himself. So perhaps it is precisely this that makes his posters so valuable to us. He is a graphic designer who devotes himself to posters with every fibre of his being, thus creating new impetus and a new justification for the latently anachronistic medium. So let us give him another commission (but not make it too easy) and let us allow him some time (but not too generously) – so that much can promise even more!

Felix Studinka

2 **54. Puce Aarberg**
54th Flea Market Aarberg
2003

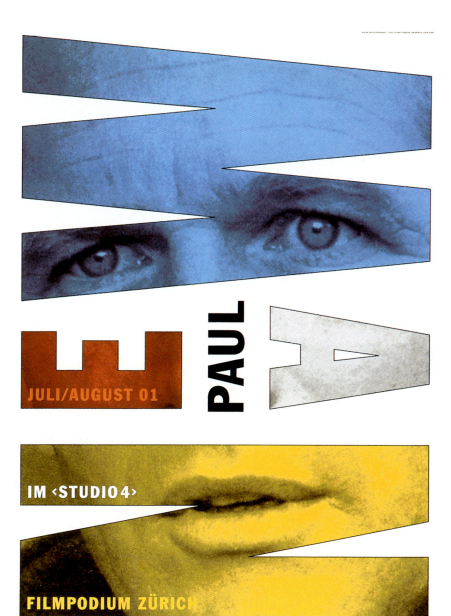

3 **Paul Newman/Filmpodium**
2001

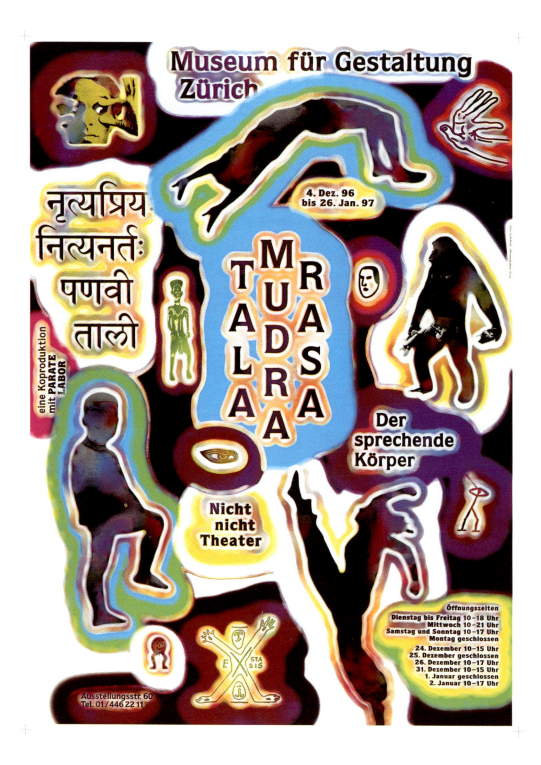

4 Tala Mudra Rasa / Museum für Gestaltung Zürich
1996

Juli Aug. 98
im <Studio 4>
Filmpodium Züri
Woody Allen
Nüschelerstr. 11

5 Woody Allen / Filmpodium
1998

6 Gross & klein / Museum für Gestaltung Zürich
Large & small
1997

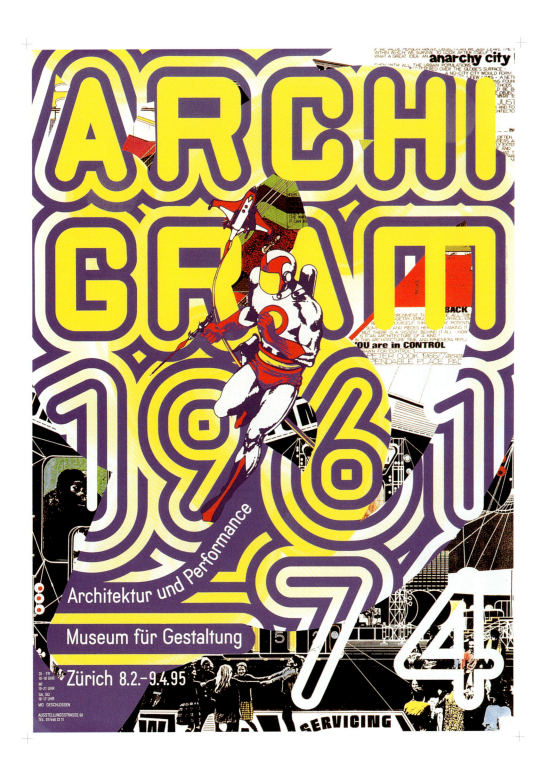

7 **Archigram / Museum für Gestaltung Zürich**
1995

Ralph Schraivogel wurde 1960 in Luzern geboren. Seine Eltern, die seine Begabung wohl gespürt haben, ermutigten ihn sich der Grafik zuzuwenden. Ab 1978 besuchte er vier Jahre die Schule für Gestaltung in Zürich. Die Rivalität zwischen den Schulen von Zürich und Basel ist bekannt, wie auch die formale Strenge und Qualität der dortigen Ausbildung bekannt ist und so Richtlinien folgt, die verschiedene Schulen geprägt haben, nicht zuletzt das Bauhaus.

Sieht man sich die Arbeit von Ralph Schraivogel jedoch genauer an, drängt sich die Frage auf, ob er den schulischen Zwang nicht eher widerstrebend über sich ergehen liess, wie Klee und Kandinsky, die ihre Lehrtätigkeit am Bauhaus, das jede kleinste seiner Regeln zum Dogma erhoben hatte, nicht fortsetzen mochten. Zu diesem Thema befragt, vermeidet Schraivogel eine Antwort oder er tut so, als habe er die Frage nicht verstanden.

Dennoch lehrt er, nach der Gründung seines eigenen Grafikateliers im Jahr 1982, seit 1992 an der Schule für Gestaltung Zürich. Er wird Mitglied der *Alliance Graphique Internationale*, nimmt an zahlreichen Gruppenausstellungen teil, und seine Plakate werden mit vielen Preisen ausgezeichnet.

Ralph Schraivogel ist ein Künstler mit selten hohen Ansprüch-en. Er schenkt der sorgfältigen Planung und Ausführung eines Projekts so viel Aufmerksamkeit, dass er nach eigener Aus-sage nicht mehr als zwei Plakate pro Jahr hervorbringen kann. Ganz anders als etwa ein viel produzierender Chéret, angeb-lich Autor von über dreitausend Plakaten. Natürlich war das Lithoplakat zu jener Zeit gerade erst geboren, die Konkurrenz zwischen den Grafikern war noch nicht so gross wie heute, und viele Geschäfte, Nachtlokale, Varietétheater und Chansonniers wollten «ihren» Chéret haben. Wahr ist auch, dass Chéret, nach dem Vorbild von Malern und Illustratoren, seine Handschrift gefunden hatte und sich endlos wiederholte im Wissen, dass seine Kunden ihm nicht folgen würden, wenn er seinen Stil ändern sollte.

Bei Schraivogel trifft das Gegenteil zu: der Künstler scheint sich bei jeder neuen Arbeit stets aufs Neue in Frage stellen zu wollen. Dies führt zu grossen und manch-mal ein wenig irreführenden Unterschieden zwischen den Plakaten und es entsteht der Eindruck, es handle sich um Werke verschiedener Grafiker. Mal hat man es mit einem Plakat zu tun, auf dem die Typografie vorherrscht, dann wieder spielt die Illustration eine wesentliche, wenn nicht die einzige Rolle, oder aber es werden beide Register gezogen und Schrift und Bild sind eng miteinander verknüpft.

Als das schönste, das genialste unter den sozusagen «typografischen» Plakaten (auch wenn das Bild, wie wir sehen werden, dabei noch seine Rolle spielt) erscheint mir das Paul Newman gewidmete Plakat 3. Ein solcher Erfolg ist um so verdienstvoller, als Grafikliebhaber und Sammler – nachdem der Druck der großen Plakatformate dank der Einführung der Lithografie vor hundertfünfzig Jahren möglich wurde – sich bei Versteigerungen illustrierter Kompositionen (von Toulouse-Lautrec bis Cassandre, von Cappiello bis Savignac) gegenseitig überbieten. Eine der wenigen Ausnahmen ist hier das Atelier Loupot mit seinem Plakat für Saint-Raphaël Quinquina, dessen grafische Kühnheit jedoch vielleicht nur durch das Beispiel Marinettis möglich war, mit seinem Manifest *Parole in Libertà*, 1913.

Ich selbst habe auf Flohmärkten hauptsächlich typografische Plakate erstanden, die mit ihrer unendlichen Vielfalt an Schriftarten und ihrem rein schwarzen Druck auf buntem Papier überwiegend aus der «romantischen Epoche» stammen. Ich halte diese Kompositionen für Meisterwerke ihre Art, und da ich einige doppelt oder dreifach besitze, habe ich versucht sie zu verkaufen. Ohne Erfolg.

Diese Ausführungen zum Paul-Newman-Plakat waren notwendig, beweist es doch eindrücklich, wenn das überhaupt notwendig ist, wie überwältigend eine klug «organisierte» Typografie wirken kann. Als gelungenste Beispiele dieses Genres erscheinen mir das Plakat *Macbeth* (2001) von Catherine Zask oder auch *Chicago* (1987) von Philippe Apeloig und die sehr viel frühere, erstaunliche Komposition *Dada* (1951) von Paul Rand. Schraivogel bedient sich der Verwandtschaft der beiden Silben eines Wortes und spielt mit der Zweideutigkeit beim Lesen (ungewohnt vertikale Leserichtung), womit er seiner Komposition den spielerischen Charakter eines Bilderrätsels verleiht. Das New und das Man bilden die beiden Gesichter, eines Janus und es bietet sich uns noch ein dritter Aspekt: das Bild des Schauspielers. Dieses Bild hatte nach Aussage von Ralph anfangs die Grösse einer Briefmarke, ein anderes war nicht zur Hand.

Verweilen wir noch einen Moment beim Typoplakat, um auch den Erfolg von Werken zu würdigen wie *Tango* 19, wie das «D» von *Deutschland über alles* 23 (dieses letzte vielleicht ein Nachfolger des polnischen Plakats der sechziger Jahre), wie *B-4* 27 und schliesslich *Macbeth* 18 (ja, auch Ralph Schraivogel hat sein Macbeth-Plakat). Überraschend ist im Übrigen nicht nur, dass der Grafiker erst sehr spät, vor drei Jahren, zur Computertechnik gekommen ist, sondern auch, dass dieses *Newman-Plakat* das erste war, das er unter Einbezug des Computers erstellt hat, wohingegen die Schlichtheit des Ausdrucks vermuten lässt, sie sei ohne Rückgriff auf eine neue und hochentwickelte Technik ausgekommen.

Bei einem Treffen in Paris habe ich Ralph Schraivogel gefragt, wovon er – abgesehen vom Bauhaus – in seinem Schaffen beeinflusst sei (und welcher Grafiker auf der ganzen Welt, von San Francisco bis Tokyo, von London oder Paris bis Berlin, kann heute ehrlich behaupten, er sei zu keinem Zeitpunkt seiner Karriere von der Bauhauslehre geprägt worden?

Expressionismus? Nein, der hat ihn nicht wirklich beeinflusst. Japanische Graphik? Ja. Pop Art? Nein, und im Übrigen scheint er dieser Bewegung, die ihm ein wenig wie ein «Intermezzo» in der Kunst vorkommt, nur wenig Bedeutung beizumessen. Dada? Ja, gewiss. Vielleicht auch weil Dada seinen Ursprung in Zürich hatte?

Es ist Ralph Schraivogel jedoch gelungen, sich von all diesen Einflüssen geschickt zu befreien. Auch wenn sie gelegentlich sichtbar sind, wie bei dem Plakat *Archigram* 7 für das Museum für Gestaltung Zürich, spielen sie in der Komposition nur die Rolle einer Referenz, eines Pastiche. Er zwingt den Dingen ganz im Gegenteil seine eigene Sicht auf, gelegentlich auf die Gefahr hin – und er macht keinen Hehl daraus, dass dies auch schon vorgekommen ist –, dass sein Entwurf abgelehnt wird. Wie gewagt war z.B. sein Bild von Isabelle Huppert 8 für das Filmpodium-Kino der Stadt Zürich, das zwar ausgesprochen lebhaft und anziehend wirkt, der Schauspielerin jedoch nicht sehr schmeichelt, und auf jeden Fall nicht zu der Art von Darstellung gehört, wie sie die Filmverleiher für ihre Werbezwecke gerne auswählen! Ralph Schraivogel kümmert das nicht: auch wenn das Foto nicht von ihm ist, verleiht er ihm ein Schicksal, gibt ihm einen Status vergleichbar mit dem der Gesichter von Malraux oder Gide, wie sie Gisèle Freund unsterblich gemacht hat.

Das Wunderbare bei Ralph Schraivogel ist, dass es ihm gelingt mit solchen Mitteln zu überraschen, die jenen, die wir für ein erfolgreiches Plakat wählen würden, vollkommen widersprechen. So z.B. die im gängigen Sinne des Wortes «unleserliche» Illustration für das Plakat der *Alliance Graphique Internationale* 31. Wie soll man sich in diesem Wirrwarr aus zerknittertem Papier zurechtfinden? Und doch zwingt er uns einen Ausweg zu suchen, wie auch bei seinen Plakaten für die *Schule für Gestaltung Bern* 30 oder auch für die *Solothurner Literaturtage* 33.

Kommen wir aber noch einmal zu dem anderen Wunder zurück: wenn man, wie ich es in der Galerie *Anatome* in Paris konnte, die Plakate aufmerksam prüft, fragt man sich, wie mehr als zwei Drittel davon «von Hand» hergestellt werden konnten, während fast alle Grafiker auf der ganzen Welt diese Machart für prähistorisch halten? Dies setzt auf der Seite des Gestalters eine aussergewöhnliche manuelle Fertigkeit voraus, die zweifelsfrei über das hinaus geht, was an den Schulen gelehrt wird und lässt erahnen, wozu ihm der Computer nützlich sein könnte.

Ralph Schraivogel schert sich nicht um Widersprüche. Er ist dort, wo man ihn nicht erwartet, und er macht nicht das, womit man rechnet. Diese Haltung ist wohltuend, weil selten. Sein letztes Werk, das Plakat *Out of print* 17, stammt vom Mai dieses Jahres. Kann man sich etwas Schlichteres, ja Banaleres vorstellen? Aber nein, schauen Sie genau hin: die Buchstaben des Haupttitels unterscheiden sich in ihrer Schriftgrösse und nehmen leicht ab. Das Ergebnis ist eine unregelmässige typografische Komposition, die nicht erstarrt wirkt. Sie ist dynamischer, ein Spiegelbild des Lebens selbst.

Robert Massin

8 Porträt Isabelle Huppert / Filmpodium
1999

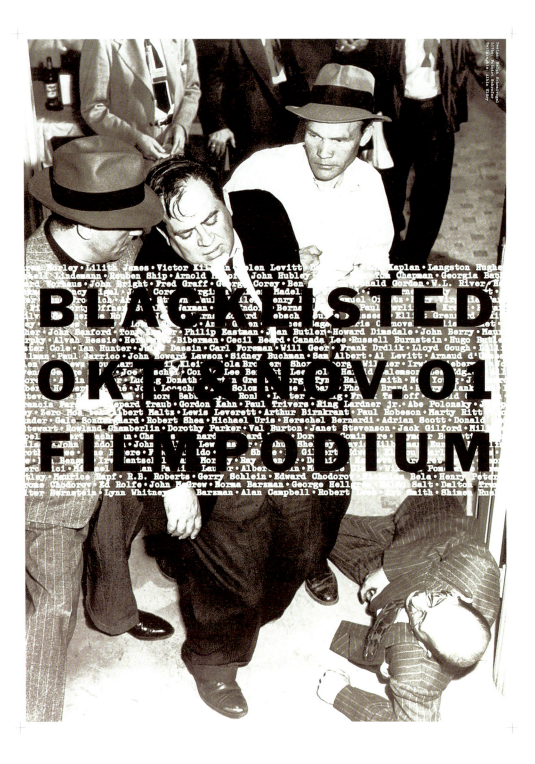

Design: Ralph Schraivogel
Litho: Michael Schnürer
Bearbeitung: Abdin Ulaç

9 **Blacklisted/Filmpodium**
2001

10 **Shakespeare's Cinema/Filmpodium**
1998

11 Stars / Filmpodium
2000

12 Chaplin / Filmpodium
1996

13 Humphrey Bogart / Marcello Mastroianni /
Filmpodium
1997

14 Palaver Palaver / Ein Film von Alexander
J. Seiler / Look Now
1990

FILMPODIUM
JULI-AUG.02

16 **John Ford/Filmpodium**
1996

Ralph Schraivogel was born in Lucerne in 1960. Detecting a certain artistic talent, his parents encouraged him to seek out a career in the graphic arts. As of 1978, he thus took up studies at Zurich's *Schule für Gestaltung*. The rivalry between the Zurich school and that of Basel is well-known, as is their high level of teaching, which embodies the strict guidelines adopted in the past by various outstanding institutions, not least of which the Bauhaus.

Yet to gaze upon Schraivogel's work is to wonder whether he was not subjected to this scholastic framework somewhat against his will, in the same fashion as Klee and Kandinsky, who so resented the dogmatism with which their own principles were applied at the Bauhaus that they gave up teaching there. When questioned in the matter, Schraivogel avoids answering, or acts as if he does not understand what is being asked.

Still and all, ten years after setting up his own graphic design studio in 1982, he himself went on to teach at the *Schule für Gestaltung Zürich*. In the meantime he had become a member of the *AGI* (Alliance Graphique Internationale), participating in many collective shows, enjoying an opportunity to have his work displayed in Osaka, and earning several prizes for his posters.

More demanding an artist than most, Schraivogel is so painstaking in the design and execution of his projects that he claims to be unable to publish more than two posters a year – a far cry from the profusion of a Jules Chéret (1836–1932), famed for some three thousand posters. Of course, at the latter's time, lithography had just come into being as a means of reproduction. Moreover, the competition was far less fierce, since not only many business firms, but also cabarets, music halls, and popular song publishers all insisted on having their "very own Chéret. Then, too, just like his fellow painters and illustrators, Chéret had found a trademark style, to which he remained steadfastly loyal, fearing that any change in manner would displease his customers and admirers.

Quite to the contrary, with every new project Schraivogel gives the impression of calling his past experience into question. Therefore, from one poster to the next, there exists great – and sometimes rather unsettling – diversity, as if different artists were involved. Sometimes the typography takes pride of place, other times the illustration. Other times still, the two are mixed, the lettering and the drawing inextricably linked. Among those of Schraivogel's posters done in what could be termed a "typographic" register (although here too the image has a role to play, as we will see), the one featuring Paul Newman 3 seems to me to be the handsomest, the most inspired. Its success is all the more noteworthy given the context: Ever since lithography made it

possible to bring out several editions of large-scale format posters – that is, for the last 150 years – print lovers and collectors who haunt the public auctions have relentlessly sought to outbid each other in a race for illustrated compositions. Many graphic artists/designers have competed for their attention, including Toulouse-Lautrec and Cappiello, Cassandre and the only recently departed Savignac. Charles Loupot's *Saint-Raphaël Quinquina*, which may well owe its graphic audacity to the precedent created by Marinetti's *Parole in libertà* (1913), represents an exception to the predominant rage for the pictorial.

At various flea markets, I myself managed to acquire several basically typographic posters, mostly from the Romantic era. Their appeal lies in the vast variety of typefaces, and the printing uniquely in black on colored paper. I value them as masterpieces of their kind. Having acquired a few of them in duplicate or even triplicate, I tried to resell them, but found no bidders.

This digression will shed light on how the Newman poster so persuasively argues, as if necessary, the tremendous impact that "skillfully arranged" typographical elements can have. I can think of few equally successful posters of this sort, except for Catherine Zask's *Macbeth* (2001) or Philippe Apeloig's *Chicago* (1987), or the amazing composition in Paul Rand's earlier *Dada* (1951) poster. Presenting a vertical reading (unusual in itself), Schraivogel's stroke of genius was to make a play on the connection between the two syllables in *Newman*, highlighting the ambiguity of their reading by introducing a playful note through the word's puzzle-like composition: "New" and "man" become the two faces of a Janus while, at the same time, the image of the actor shows through. The artist explains that, at the time, the only image of Newman available for him to work with was the size of a postage stamp!

Other posters by this artist in the same typographical vein, and that also enjoyed a good measure of success, are his *Tango* 19, the "D" in *Deutschland über alles* 23 (perhaps heir to the Polish posters of the sixties), the *B-4* poster 27, *NY* 15 and, last but not least, his *Macbeth* 18 (yes, indeed, Schraivogel too has his Macbeth). Surprisingly, Schraivogel availed himself of a computer very late in his career, a mere three years ago. No less surprising is the fact that, in its simplicity, his *Newman* poster – the first of his posters to be digitally created – looks like it could just as well have been achieved without such new and sophisticated technology.

When I once met with Schraivogel in Paris, I asked him about the various influences he might have undergone, besides that of the Bauhaus. (Since, obviously, from San Francisco to Tokyo and from London to Paris, there is hardly a graphic artist alive today who would deny having been influenced at some point by the Bauhaus.) Could it be Expressionism? No, not really, Perhaps Japanese graphic art? Yes. What about Pop? No – said in a way that reveals a certain lack of interest in this movement, considered as a sort of "interlude" in the realm of artistic creation. Dada? Yes, certainly. Maybe because Zurich (where Schraivogel is based) is the birthplace of Dada…

Be that as it may, in the meantime Schraivogel has skillfully detached himself from all these influences. The rare times they do crop up visually – his *Archigram* 7 poster for the Museum für Gestaltung Zürich comes to mind – they are not part and parcel of the composition but serve as points of reference, or even as a pastiche. Instead, he is wont to impose his own vision of things, even if this has sometimes meant, as he himself freely admits, that one project or the other invites rejection. Indeed, how audacious it was of him to propose that the poster for Zurich *Film-podium-Kino* feature a rather unflattering image of the otherwise quite endearing and vivacious French film star Isabelle Huppert 8. Not only that, but it was an image that could hardly appeal to the film distribution world for promotional purposes. Schraivogel stood his ground: the photo may not have been by him, but it is he who deliberately brought it into the limelight, granting it a status on a level with the faces of Malraux or Gide that Gisèle Freund so artfully captured and immortalized.

Miraculously, this graphic designer is often at his most convincing when applying methods that contradict his recommendations. Consider the almost "illegible"– in the ordinary sense of the term – wording in the *Alliance Graphique Internationale* 31 poster. How can we possibly make it out from amidst all that muddle of wrinkled paper? In fact, he forces us to find a solution, exactly as he does with his *Schule for Gestaltung Bern* 30 or *Solothurner Literaturtage* 33 posters.

Another miracle: Three-quarters of all the posters he displayed at the Galerie *Anatome* in Paris, which I had occasion to carefully examine, were done "by hand", and this in an era when almost all his peers have relegated such an approach to prehistory. This implies both that the artist possesses the sort of extraordinary manual skill that no school can teach, and that he somehow intuited all that computers would someday have to contribute to his work.

Then again, this is a graphic designer who revels in contradictions, most likely to be found where you would least expect him to be and doing what, in all logic, you would least expect him to do. It is a praiseworthy attitude because it is so uncommon. Not only is he willing to take risks, but also to accept the consequences. His most recent creation dates to last May: the *Out of print* 17 poster. What could be simpler, almost prosaic...? Take another look, and you will notice that the body sizes in the lettering of the main title all differ slightly, *diminuendo*. The resulting typographic composition is not regular or rigidified: It is thus more dynamic, and is in the image of life itself.

Robert Massin

DESIGN: RALPH SCHRAIVOGEL (SEROGRAPHIE: KOPP)

OUT OF PRINT

ARCHIVE FOR SMALL PRESS
& COMMUNICATION 1960–1980
MUSEUM FÜR GESTALTUNG
ZÜRICH 1. MÄRZ–18. MAI 2003
DIENSTAG–DONNERSTAG 10–20
FREITAG–SONNTAG 11–16
MONTAG GESCHLOSSEN
AUSSTELLUNGSSTRASSE 60
CH–8005 ZÜRICH

17 **Out of print / Museum für Gestaltung Zürich**
2003

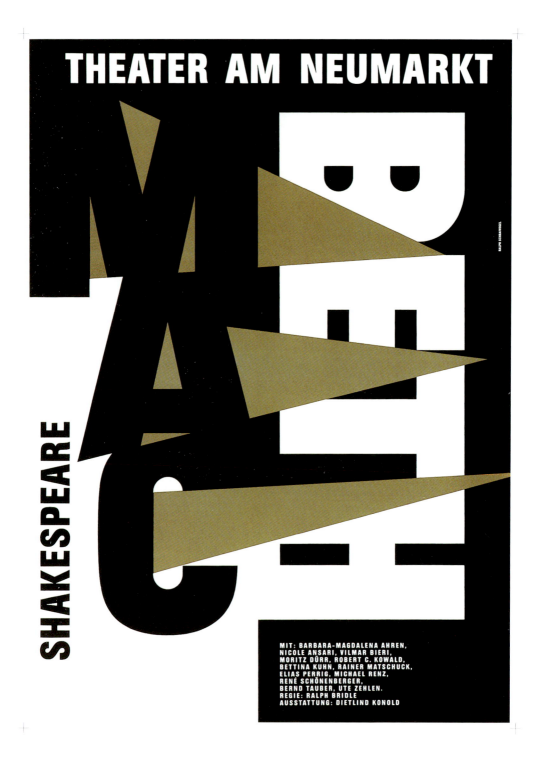

THEATER AM NEUMARKT

MACBETH

SHAKESPEARE

MIT: BARBARA-MAGDALENA AHREN,
NICOLE ANSARI, VILMAR BIERI,
MORITZ DÜRR, ROBERT C. KOWALD,
BETTINA KUHN, RAINER MATSCHUCK,
ELIAS PERRIG, MICHAEL RENZ,
RENÉ SCHÖNENBERGER,
BERND TAUBER, UTE ZEHLEN.
REGIE: RALPH BRIDLE
AUSSTATTUNG: DIETLIND KONOLD

18 Macbeth/Theater am Neumarkt
1990

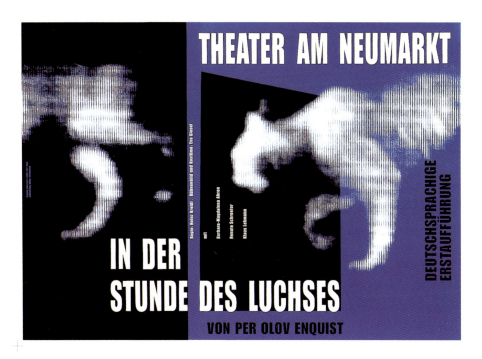

19 Tango / Theater am Neumarkt
1990

20 In der Stunde des Luchses / Theater am Neumarkt
In the hour of the lynx
1990

21 Der Wilde Mann / Ein Film von Matthias Zschokke / Look Now
The Wild Man
1989

22 Tie-Break für Crazy Horse / Theater am Neumarkt
1990

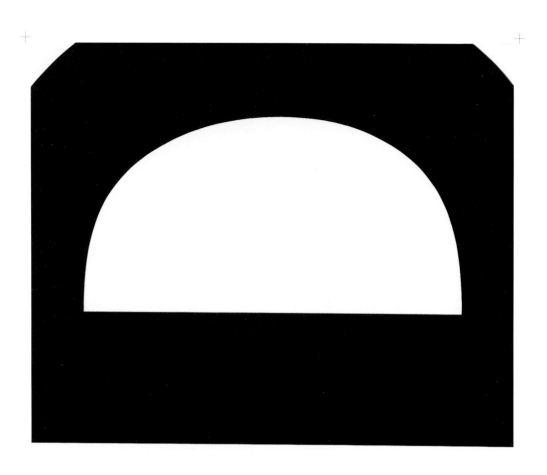

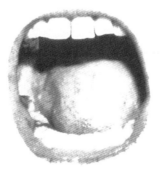

«DEUTSCHLAND
ÜBER ALLES»

23 «Deutschland über alles»
1994

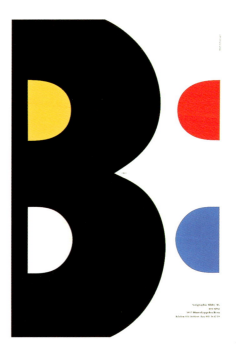

24 Im Rückenwind/Museum für Gestaltung Zürich
With Tailwind
1990

25 Remmidemmi aus Burundi/Museum für
Gestaltung Zürich – Rumpus from Burundi
1985

26 «Für eine Zukunft mit Zukunft»
"For a future with future"
1990

27 B-4/Serigraphie Uldry AG
1992

28 **Die Welt im Kasten / Strauhof Zürich**
The world in the box
1994

29 **Jazzfestival Schaffhausen**
2002

EIN JAZZ SOLO
Felix Studinka

Das Plakat ist ein Medium, in dem das Sehen und das Lesen in ein wirksames Verhältnis treten. Ralph Schraivogel scheint dieses Verhältnis immer wieder an einen Punkt führen zu wollen, wo Schrift ebenso gesehen, Form ebenso gelesen wird. Er bewegt sich nicht auf einem Weg, der linear vom grafischen Einfall zur Ausführung führt, sondern er begibt sich bewusst auf unvorhersehbare Irr- und Umwege. Mit seiner komplexen und zeitraubenden Arbeitsweise leistet er sich eine Exklusivität, die ihn jedoch keineswegs in Verlegenheit bringt: Auf die lange Entstehungszeit seiner Plakate angesprochen, zitiert Schraivogel David Hockney, der einmal gesagt haben soll, dass man einer Sache ansähe, wie lange sie betrachtet worden ist. Solche Bedachtsamkeit überrascht im Bereich des «schnellen» Mediums Plakat und verrät einen Anspruch, der weit über die primären Erfordernisse der Werbung hinausgeht. Seine Methode erfordert, dass sich das Gestalten und das Betrachten in kleinsten Zyklen abwechseln. Dieser Prozess wird durch eine atemberaubende Menge von Skizzen und Computerausdrucken protokolliert, die sich über Boden und Wände des Ateliers ausbreitet.

Nehmen wir das Plakat für das Schaffhauser Jazzfestival. Das avantgardistische Selbstverständnis der Auftraggeber und ihre Toleranz in bezug auf die visuelle Kommunikation sind keineswegs Voraussetzungen, die gute Ergebnisse garantieren, aber sie kommen Schraivogels Arbeitsweise entgegen. Bis auf den Text gab es für das Plakat keinerlei Vorgaben – eine Ausgangslage, die er nutzt, um die Gefahr einer übereilten Lösung zu zerstreuen und stattdessen durch die ziellose Beschäftigung mit banalen Kritzeleien das kreative Tempo anzugeben. Er sucht keine visuellen Analogien zur Musik. Aber er versetzt sich – durchaus vergleichbar mit der musikalischen Improvisation – in eine schöpferische Unruhe, in der die Intuition dem Gedanken vorausgeht und die grafischen Akkorde und Rhythmen hervorbringt. Es sammeln sich Notizen an, in denen das Wort «Jazz» auf seine typografische Energie geprüft wird. Angezogen vom Paradox des Wortes, entfremdet er sich von seinem Sinn und führt es in eine krude dreidimensionale Form. Die dreimalige Biegung des Buchstabens «Z» erregt kurz seine Aufmerksamkeit, aber sie wird bald auf neue Spuren gelenkt. Schraivogel erinnert sich an eine Figuration, auf die er schon vor Jahren gestossen war: Ein nudelartiges Wirrwarr von Linien, entstanden durch die Misshandlung eines Faxpapiers mit dem Lötkolben, gibt ihm Rätsel auf, die ihn zur weiteren Beschäftigung antreiben. Kein Ansatz ist im Anfangsstadium absurd genug, um die Sinne anzuregen: Wie die meisten Skizzen bleibt auch das durch den Scanner gezogene, wacklige Bild einer Hand, deren Fingerspitzen als «Z» lesbar werden, ein verworfener Solitär.

«Zerstörung-Wiederherstellung» findet man auf einer der Skizzen notiert: die Ermahnung, seine Gedanken in Bewegung zu halten. Er sucht die Entfremdung, indem er zufällige Formen so lange misshandelt und verunreinigt, bis sie ein inneres Einverständnis auslösen und den folgenden Schritt zur Notwendigkeit machen. Schraivogels Lust auf unerwartete Seherlebnisse hat sich noch verstärkt, seit er am Computer arbeitet: Hier wird der Buchstabe «Z» zum Vorwand für unzählige zu neuen Recherchen anregende digitale Morphs. Von den

zerfetzten Morphs geblieben sind dynamische Kraftlinien, die sich erneut mit typografischen Elementen versetzen. Das Prinzip solcher Erkundungen ist auch in anderen Plakaten evident: Das je von Typografie und Form beanspruchte Vorrecht Schicht um Schicht zu beruhigen, bis sie ihre Konkurrenz aufgeben. Die Linien werden nun mit den Namen aller am Festival beteiligten Musiker besetzt. Das Spiel wird erprobt, doch aufs Neue verknäueln sich Schrift und Bild: Die Buchstaben der Namen gerinnen zu unlesbaren Flecken und mutieren schliesslich zu Haarlinien, die sich zu flimmernden Bändern formieren. Der Gestalter mag Tage und Wochen mit solchen Experimenten zugebracht haben, doch allmählich verändert sich der zyklische Prozess von Verdichtung und Verflüssigung, von Verwunderung und Beherrschung.

Eine röhrenförmige Struktur beginnt zu greifen und führt den Entwurf von der Breite in die Tiefe. Von nun an wird die gedankliche Vorwegnahme des Druckprozesses in die Gestaltung mit einbezogen. Probeweise werden die Schläuche zum Wort «Jazz» arrangiert und das Wort überlebt nur noch als Erinnerung in einem immer verschlungener werdenden Muster von Röhren. Ihnen werden nun ausladende Studien gewidmet, um sie mit Kontrasten anzureichern. Man beginnt jetzt zu begreifen, dass Ralph Schraivogel mit der Sorgfalt eines Ingenieurs eine räumliche Logik der durcheinander gewundenen Röhren herstellt. Während sie sich zu einem kompositorischen Gerüst festigen, werden Detailstudien für die gegenseitigen Interferenzen von Schrift und Hintergrund angefertigt.

In einer anderen Untersuchung vertieft er sich in die Farboptionen des Siebdrucks. Mit Hilfe einer ausufernden Kombinatorik gilt es nicht nur zu entscheiden, welche Elemente in Schwarz, Weiss oder Silber gedruckt werden sollen, sondern auch in welcher Reihenfolge und in wie vielen Durchgängen. Hier zeigt sich, was er – nebst dem Provozieren produktiver Störfälle – am Computer besonders schätzt, nämlich die Perfektion, mit der er die visuellen Fundstücke organisieren und am ausgedruckten Blatt überprüfen kann. Kein Wunder, dass auch von seinem bewährten Drucker Albin Uldry das Äusserste abverlangt wird. Der Druck ist die Hauptprobe des Arrangements, denn was in vielen Einzelschritten eingeübt worden ist, lässt nur noch geringe Korrekturen zu.

Im Mai 2002 erscheint auf Schaffhausens Strassen ein seltsam schwereloses Musikplakat, das sich in seinen Details nicht erschöpft, so nahe man auch herantritt. Sein dominierendes Motiv und die vibrierenden Variationen rieseln ineinander: Wie das gleichnamige Plakat von 1997, und doch ganz anders, ist es «gross und klein».

A JAZZ SOLO
Felix Studinka

The poster is a medium in which seeing and reading enter into an potent relationship. Ralph Schraivogel seems to have only one aim in this respect: taking that relationship to a point where lettering is seen in exactly the same way and form is read in exactly the same way. He does not move along a linear path from a graphic idea to its execution, but deliberately sets off on unpredictable wrong tracks and detours. His complex and time-consuming approach gives him an exclusive quality that does not embarrass him at all: when asked why his posters take so long, Schraivogel cites David Hockney, who apparently once said that you can see from a thing how long it has been looked at. This level of deliberation is surprising in the "speedy" world of the poster, and betrays an ambition that goes well beyond the primary demands of advertising. His method requires that creativity and consideration alternate in the tiniest of cycles. This process is recorded in a breathtaking number of sketches and computer print-outs, spreading over the floor and walls of the studio.

Let us take the poster for the Schaffhausen Jazz Festival. The clients' avant-garde self-perception and their tolerance vis-à-vis visual communication by no means guarantee good results, but they suit Schraivogel's working methods. Nothing was laid down for the posters except the text – a starting-point he uses to dissipate the danger of an over-hasty solution, instead setting the creative tempo by aimlessly occupying himself with banal scribblings. He is not looking for visual analogies with music. But he places himself – and this is entirely comparable with musical improvisation – in a state of creative unrest in which intuition precedes thought and produces graphic chords and rhythms. He accumulates notes in which the word "jazz" is tested for typographical energy. Attracted by the paradox of the word, he distances himself from its meaning and shifts it into a crude three-dimensional form. His attention is caught briefly by the three bends in the letter "Z", but it is soon diverted elsewhere. Schraivogel recalls a configuration he came across years ago: a noodle-like entanglement of lines created by maltreating fax paper with a soldering iron sets him some puzzles that stimulate further activity. In the early stages, no approach is absurd enough to get him going: like most sketches, the wobbly, scanned image of a hand whose fingertips can be read as a "Z" ends up as a rejected singleton as well.

"Destruction-recomposition" reads the note on one of the sketches: reminding him to keep his thoughts moving. He is looking for alienation by maltreating and polluting random forms for so long that they trigger an inner agreement and make the next step a necessity. Schraivogel's delight in unexpected visual experiences has become all the stronger since he has started using a computer: here the letter "Z" becomes a pretext for countless digital morphs that stimulate new research. What remains of the ripped up morphs are dynamic force-lines that again mingle with typographical elements. This kind of exploratory principle is also evident in other posters: the aim is to smooth out the privilege claimed by both typography and form layer by layer, until they stop competing with each other. The lines are now occupied by the names of all the musicians taking part in the festival. This game is tried out, but again script and image become entangled: the letters of the names develop into illegible spots and ultimately mutate into hairlines that form shimmering bands. The designer may have spent days and weeks on experiments like this, but the cyclical process of condensation and liquefaction, of surprise and control, is gradually changing.

A tubular structure starts to exert its grip, and shifts the design from breadth into depth. From now on, intellectual anticipation of the printing process becomes part of the design. The tubes are tentatively arranged to form the word "Jazz", and the word then survives only as a memory in an increasingly tangled pattern of tubes. These now become the subject of extensive studies in which they are enriched with contrast. We are now beginning to understand that Ralph Schraivogel is using an engineer's precision to create a three-dimensional logic for the tubes as they curve around each other. Detailed studies are prepared for the mutual interference of lettering and background as they settle into a compositional framework. He launches another investigation to explore the colour options provided by screen printing. An elaborate ars combinatoria is called upon not just to decide which elements should be printed in black, white or silver, but also in what sequence and how many times over. Here we can see – apart from provoking productive faults – what he particularly likes about the computer: the perfection with which it can organize visual found objects and test them on a printed sheet. No wonder, that he also demands the utmost from his tried-and-tested printer Albin Uldry. Printing is the dress rehearsal for the arrangement, as something that has been prepared in a number of individual steps admits only minimal correction.

In May 2002 a strangely weightless music poster appeared in the streets of Schaffhausen, inexhaustible in its detail however close you got to it. Its dominant motif and the vibrant variations trickle into each other: like the 1997 poster of the same name, and yet quite different, it is "large and small".

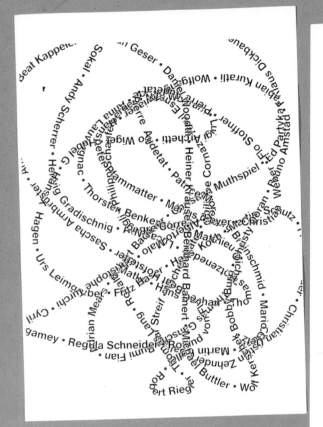

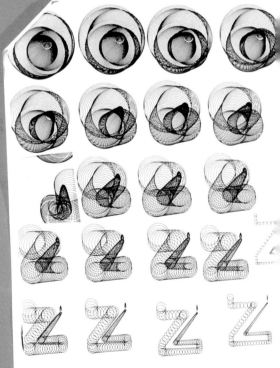

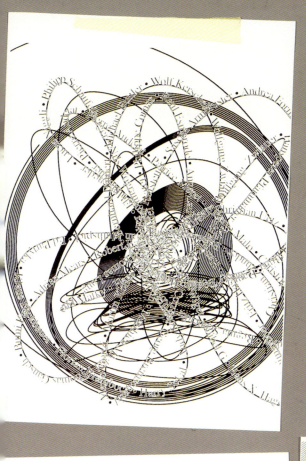

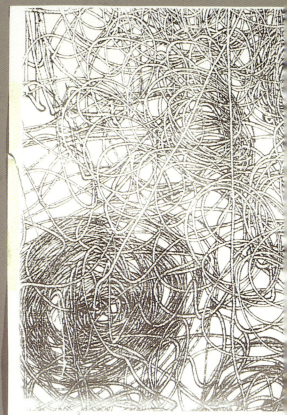

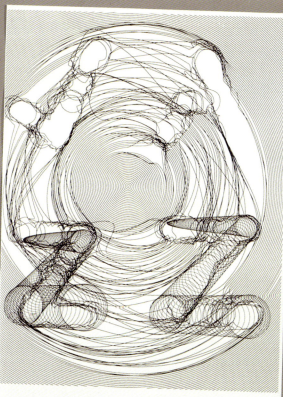

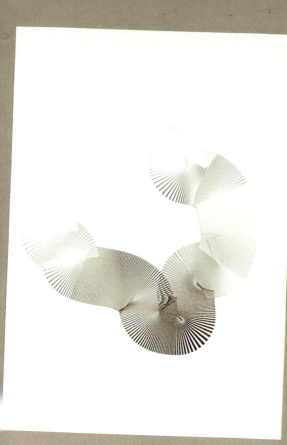

Christian Zehnder • Baltasar Streit • Michel Batet

Christian Zehnder • Baltasar Streit • Michel Batet • Philippe Cornaz

Christian Zehnder Zehnder

Michel

Christian Zehnder • Baltasar Streit • Michel Batet • Phi

13. S... ...us.

Jazz... ...sti...

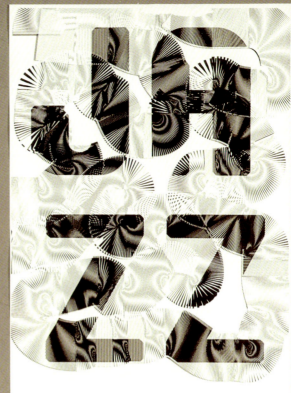

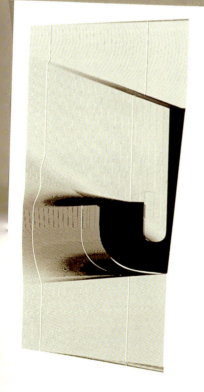

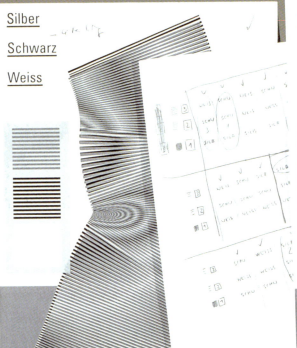

Silber

Schwarz

Weiss

Weiss

Schwarz

Weiss

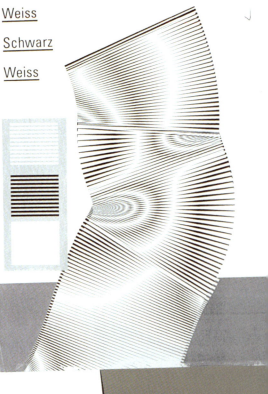

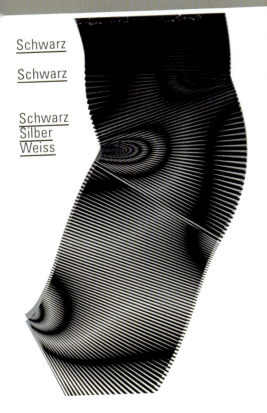

Schwarz

Schwarz

Schwarz
Silber
Weiss

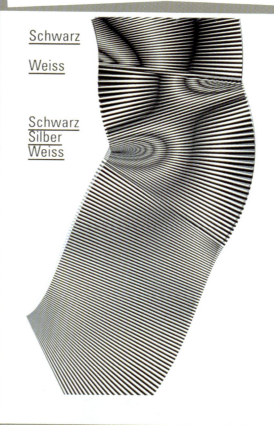

Schwarz

Weiss

Schwarz
Silber
Weiss

A Merf 4 Merf Kopie 15

K — Merf → N

30 **Ralph Schraivogel Plakate/Schule für Gestaltung Bern**
1998

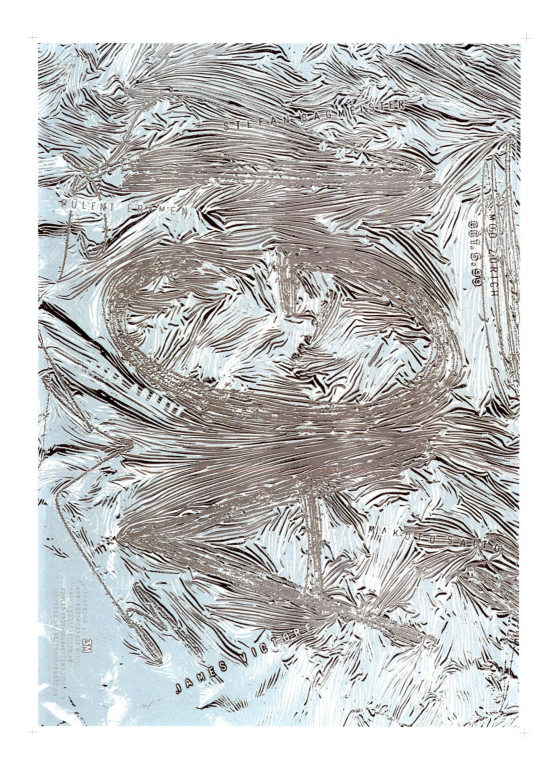

31 **AGI Seminar Zurich / Alliance Graphique Internationale**
1999

32 **Int. Jazz-Festival / Reithalle Gessnerallee**
1989

Solothurner Literaturtage 1996

Journées Littéraires de Soleure

Giornate

Giornate Letterarie di Soletta

Giornate Letterari di Soletta

Sentupada Litterara a Soletta

Sentupada Litterara a Soloturn

33 Solothurner Literaturtage
The Solothurn Literature Days
1996

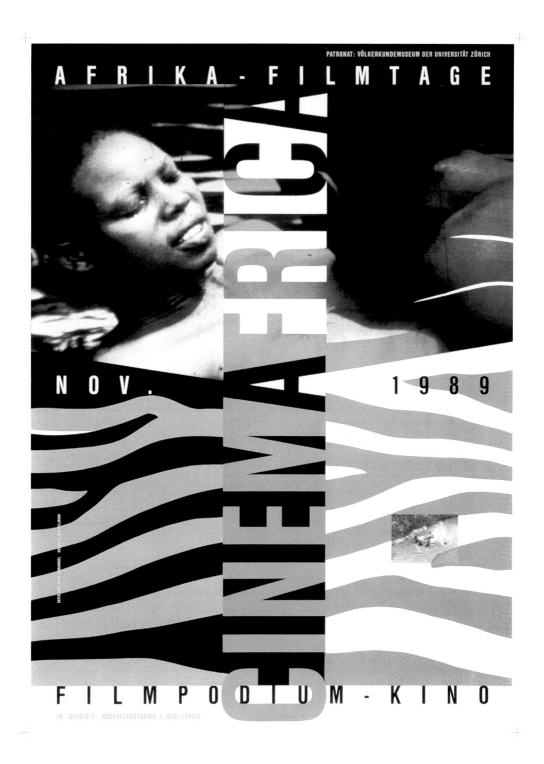

34 Cinémafrica/Afrika-Filmtage/Filmpodium
1989

35 **Cinémafrica / Afrika-Filmtage / Filmpodium**
1991

36 **Cinémafrica / Afrika-Filmtage / Filmpodium**
1993

"STUDIO 4"
Nüschelerstr. 11
Zürich

37 Cinémafrica / Afrika-Filmtage / Filmpodium
1995

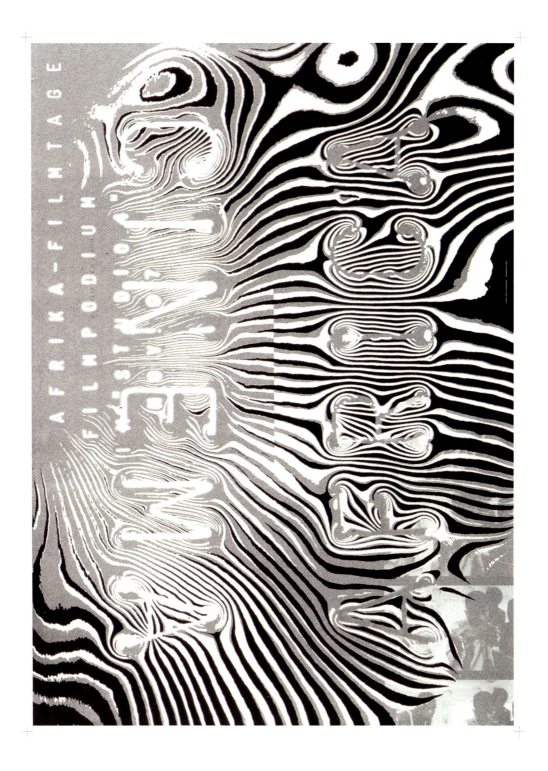

38 **Cinémafrica / Afrika-Filmtage / Filmpodium**
1997

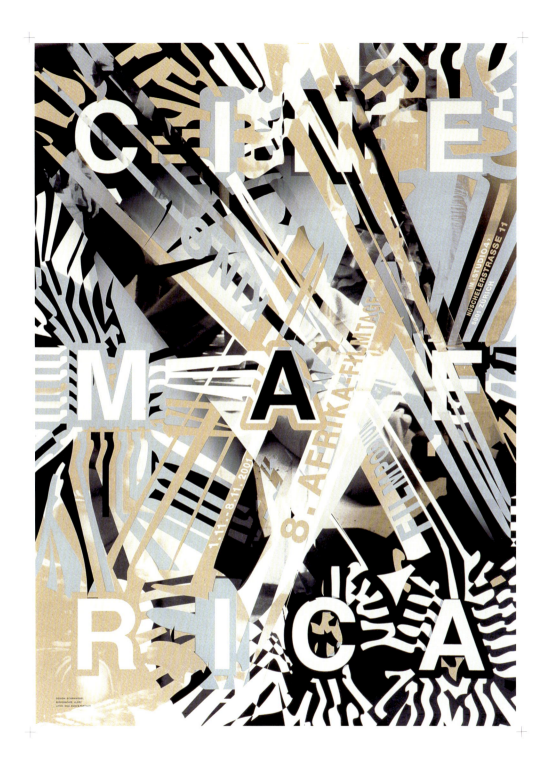

39 **Cinémafrica / Afrika-Filmtage / Filmpodium**
2001

Kurzbiografie

Ralph Schraivogel, geboren 1960 in Luzern (Schweiz) wird 1977 bis 1982 an der Schule für Gestaltung Zürich zum Grafiker ausgebildet. Seit dem Ende des Studiums arbeitet er als selbständiger Grafiker in Zürich. Neben der Gestaltung von verschiedenen Akzidenzen, Logos und Erscheinungsbildern widmet er sich vor allem dem Kulturplakat. Für das Zürcher Studio-Kino Filmpodium entstehen seit 1983 Plakate und Programmzeitschriften; vom Museum für Gestaltung Zürich erhält er seit 1984 wiederholt Aufträge für Plakate und Einladungskarten. Zwischen 1986 und 1989 entstehen im Auftrag des Kunsthauses Zürich Kataloge und Plakate, 1991 eine Reihe von Plakaten für das Theater am Neumarkt in Zürich. Seit Beginn der neunziger Jahre wird Ralph Schraivogel im In- und Ausland mit zahlreichen Auszeichnungen für seine Plakate geehrt und der Kreis der Kunden weitet sich aus: es entstehen Arbeiten für das Jazzfestival Zürich, das Schaffhauser Jazzfestival, die Solothurner Literaturtage und das Festival des Afrikanischen Films in Zürich, Cinémafrica. Zehn Jahre nach seinem Studienabschluss kehrt Schraivogel als Dozent an die Schule für Gestaltung Zürich zurück, wo er bis 2001 unterrichtet. Daneben erhält er Lehraufträge in Bremen und Berlin und leitet Workshops in Europa und den USA. Mehrere Einzelausstellungen, u.a. in Warschau, Osaka, Teheran, Paris und Hangzhou, bringen sein Plakatwerk einem grossen Publikum näher. Er ist Mitglied der Alliance Graphique Internationale, AGI.

Biography

Ralph Schraivogel was born in 1960 in Lucerne (Switzerland). He trained as a graphic artist at the Schule für Gestaltung Zürich from 1977 to 1982. He has worked in Zurich as a free-lance graphic artist since graduating. He designs jobbing work, logos and corporate identities, but devotes himself above all to cultural posters. He has created posters and programme magazines for the Zürcher art-house cinema Filmpodium since 1983; he has repeatedly had posters and invitation cards commissioned by the Museum für Gestaltung Zürich since 1984. Catalogues and posters were designed for the Kunsthaus Zürich from 1986 to 1989, and a series of posters for the Theater am Neumarkt in Zurich in 1991. Ralph Schraivogel has received various awards for his posters at home and abroad since the early nineties, and his client circle is expanding: work is being produced for the Zurich Jazz Festival, the Schaffhausen Jazz Festival, the Solothurn Literature Days and Cinémafrica, the African Film Festival in Zurich. Ten years after graduating, Schraivogel returned to the Schule für Gestaltung in Zurich as a lecture, and taught there until 2001. He has also held teaching posts in Bremen and Berlin and directs workshops in Europe and the USA. Several one-man shows, in locations including Warsaw, Osaka, Teheran, Paris and Hangzhou, have introduced his poster work to a wider public. He is a member of the Alliance Graphique Internationale, AGI.

Jacques Uldry, Albin Ulrdry, Ralph Schraivogel bei Serigraphie Uldry AG in Hinterkappelen (Bern). Besprechung beim Druck des Plakates «54. Puce Aarberg», 2003.
Foto: Dominique Uldry

Jacques Uldry, Albin Uldry, Ralph Schraivogel at Serigraphie Uldry AG in Hinterkappelen (Bern). Discussion at the printing of the "54. Puce Aarberg" poster, 2003.
Photograph: Dominique Uldry

Katalog

Die abgebildeten Plakate stammen alle aus der Plakatsammlung des Museums für Gestaltung Zürich.

Die Daten des Katalogs folgen den Rubriken Plakattext, Erscheinungsjahr, Drucktechnik und Format. Dabei gelten folgende Regelungen:

Plakattext: Die beste Textwiedergabe bildet die Abbildung des Plakates selbst. Darum wird hier eine vereinfachte Form wiedergegeben, welche nur die aussagekräftigsten Textbestandteile berücksichtigt. Allfällige Umstellungen dienen der Verständlichkeit. Das Zeichen / trennt inhaltliche Texteinheiten.

Drucktechnik: Die englische Übersetzung der Drucktechnik erschliesst sich meist aus dem deutschen Begriff.

Format: Die Angaben werden in der Abfolge Höhe × Breite und in cm gemacht. Weil die Plakate nicht immer exakt rechtwinklig geschnitten sind, werden die Abmessungen auf halbe cm aufgerundet.

Die Plakatgeschichte ist ein junges Forschungsgebiet – verlässliche Informationen sind rar. Jeder Hinweis und jede Ergänzung sind willkommen: plakat.sammlung@museum-gestaltung.ch.

Catalogue

The posters illustrated come from the Museum für Gestaltung Zürich's Poster Collection.

The data in the catalogue are under the headings poster text, year of appearance, country of first appearance, printing technique, format. The following rules have been applied:

Poster text: the poster itself provides the best version of the text. Thus a simplified form is used here, giving only the most meaningful elements of the text. Any rearrangements that have been made are for purposes of intelligibility. The sign / separates textual units by content.

Printing technique: the English translation of the printing technique is usually suggested by the German concept, as in Offset. Siebdruck means Screenprint.

Format: the details are given in the sequence height × width and in cm. Because the posters are often not cut exactly at right angles, the dimensions are rounded off to half cm.

The history of posters is a recent field of research – reliable information is rare. Any references or additional material are welcome: plakat.sammlung@museum-gestaltung.ch

1 Henry van de Velde/
Museum für Gestaltung Zürich
Foto: Peter Lüem
1993
Siebdruck 128 × 90,5

2 54. Puce Aarberg/
Organisation Aarberger Puce
54th Flea Market Aarberg
2003
Siebdruck 128 × 90,5

3 Paul Newman/Filmpodium
2001
Siebdruck 128 × 90,5

4 Tala Mudra Rasa/
Der sprechende Körper/
Museum für Gestaltung Zürich
The speaking body
1996
Siebdruck 128 × 90,5

5 Woody Allen/Filmpodium
1998
Siebdruck 128 × 90,5

6 Gross & klein/
Museum für Gestaltung Zürich
Large & small
Foto: Peter Hunkeler
1997
Siebdruck 128 × 90,5

7 Archigram/
Museum für Gestaltung Zürich
1995
Siebdruck 128 × 90,5

8 Porträt Isabelle Huppert/
Filmpodium
1999
Siebdruck 128 × 90,5

9 Blacklisted/Filmpodium
2001
Siebdruck 128 × 90,5

10 Shakespeare's Cinema/
Filmpodium
1998
Siebdruck 128 × 90,5

11 Sie leuchten noch heute/
Stars von gestern/Filmpodium
2000
Siebdruck 128 × 90,5

12 Chaplin/
Filmpodium
1996
Siebdruck 128 × 90,5

13 Humphrey Bogart/
Marcello Mastroianni/Filmpodium
1997
Siebdruck 128 × 90,5

14 Palaver Palaver/Ein Film von
Alexander J. Seiler/Look Now
1990
Offset 59,4 × 42

15 NY/Filmpodium
2002
Siebdruck 128 × 90,5

16 John Ford/Filmpodium
1996
128 × 90,5

17 Out of print/
Museum für Gestaltung Zürich
2003
Siebdruck 128 × 90,5

18 Macbeth/
Theater am Neumarkt
1990
Offset 59 × 42

19 Tango/Theater am Neumarkt
1990
Offset 42 × 59

20 In der Stunde des Luchses/
Theater am Neumarkt
In the hour of the lynx
1990
Offset 42 × 59

21 Der Wilde Mann/ Ein Film von
Matthias Zschokke/Look Now
The Wild Man
1989
Offset 42 × 59

22 Tie-Break für Crazy Horse/
Theater am Neumarkt
1990
Offset 42 × 59

23 «Deutschland über alles»
1994
Siebdruck 84 × 59

24 Im Rückenwind/
Die StipendiatInnen des
Eidgenössischen Stipendiums für
angewandte Kunst 1990/
Museum für Gestaltung Zürich
With Tailwind
1991
Siebdruck 128 × 90,5

25 Remmidemmi aus Burundi/
Museum für Gestaltung Zürich
Rumpus from Burundi
1985
Offset 128 × 90,5

26 «Für eine Zukunft mit Zukunft»
Projekt der Stiftung für engagierte
visuelle Kommunikation im Rah-
men des Festes der vier Kulturen
"For a future with future"

Foto: Peter Hunkeler
1990
Siebdruck 128 × 90,5

27 B-4/Serigraphie Uldry AG
1992
Siebdruck 128 × 90,5

28 Die Welt im Kasten/
[Museum] Strauhof Zürich
The world in the box
1994
Siebdruck 128 × 90,5

29 Jazzfestival Schaffhausen
2002
Siebdruck 128 × 90,5

30 Ralph Schraivogel Plakate/
Schule für Gestaltung Bern
1998
Siebdruck 84 × 59

31 AGI Seminar Zurich/
Alliance Graphique Internationale
1999
Siebdruck

32 Int. Jazz-Festival/
Reithalle Gessnerallee
Foto: Peter Hunkeler
1989
Siebdruck 128 × 90,5

33 Solothurner Literaturtage
The Solothurn Literature Days
1996
Siebdruck 128 × 90,5

34 Cinémafrica/Afrika-Filmtage/
Filmpodium
1989
Siebdruck 128 × 90,5

35 Cinémafrica/Afrika-Filmtage/
Filmpodium
1991
Siebdruck 128 × 90,5

36 Cinémafrica/Afrika-Filmtage/
Filmpodium
1993
Siebdruck 128 × 90,5

37 Cinémafrica/Afrika-Filmtage/
Filmpodium
1995
Siebdruck 128 x 90,5

38 Cinémafrica/Afrika-Filmtage/
Filmpodium
1997
Siebdruck 128 x 90,5

39 Cinémafrica/Afrika-Filmtage/
Filmpodium
2001
Siebdruck 128 x 90,5

Robert Massin, geboren 1925, lebt in Paris.
Als *Grafiker* und Typograf debütierte er in den 50-er
Jahren in Buchklubs, wo er eine ganz wesentliche Rolle
bei der Revolutionierung der Buchgestaltung spielte.
Ab 1958 war er während zwanzig Jahren künstlerischer
Direktor bei Gallimard. Als freier Grafiker entwarf
er tausende von Buchumschlägen, und war verantwort-
lich für das Entstehen zahlreicher Illustrationen und
Plakate.
Als *Journalist* interviewte er als erster Céline, als dieser
1947 in Dänemark aus der Haft entlassen wurde,
und als Einziger traf er Malcolm Lowry als «Under the
Volcano» in Frankreich erschien.
Als *Verleger* führte er eine Zeit lang das Atelier
Hachette/Massin, beim dem, so ein Kritiker, «aussergewöhnliche und herrliche Bücher» erschienen sind.
Als Schriftsteller veröffentlichte er 1970 «La Lettre
et l'image» mit einem Vorwort von Queneau und einem
Kommentar von Roland Barthes, wofür er den *Prix
des Graphistes* erhielt, und das in die «Bibliothèque
idéale» aufgenommen wurde. Darüber hinaus ist er
Autor von Werken über die Geschichte der Stadt Paris
(«Les Cris de la ville»); «Zola photographe» sowie
von theoretischen Schriften und ästhetischen Reflexio-
nen über die Grafik oder die Interaktion der Künste:
«L'ABC du Métier», Imprimerie Nationale; «La Mise
en pages», Hoëbeke; «De la variation», Le Promeneur;
«Style et écriture», Albin Michel.
Als *Tagebuchschreiber* veröffentlichte er «Continuo»,
bei Seuil und «Journal en désordre» bei Robert Laffont.
Als *Musikfan* arbeitete er bei Musiksendungen des
Senders France Musique mit.
Als *Illustrator* schuf er Bücher mit Collagen nach Texten
von Prévert, Gallimard.
Als *Fotograf* veröffentlichte er bei Hoëbeke ein Buch
über Picassiette.
Massin schreibt auch unter dem Pseudonym Claude
Menuet. Sein wirkungsvolles und breites kulturelles
Schaffen ist Gegenstand vielfacher Auseinandersetzung
und Auszeichnung.

Robert Massin, born in 1925. Lives in Paris.
As a graphic designer and typographer... Massin began
in book clubs, playing a leading role in the '50s
movement revolutionizing book design. In 1958 he
began a 20-year stint as artistic director at Gallimard.
His freelance commissions include countless
book covers, illustrated publication layouts, and posters.
As a *journalist...* He was the first to interview Céline
upon the latter's release from prison in Denmark
in 1947, and the only one to meet Malcolm Lowry when
"Under the Volcano" came out in France.
As an *editor...* For several years he directed the Atelier
Hachette/Massin, publishing what one critic, termed
"extraordinary and superb books."
As a *writer...* In 1970, his "La Lettre et l'image", prefaced
by Queneau and with a commentary by Roland Barthes,
was published; it received the Prix des Graphistes
and became listed in the "Bibliothèque idéale".
He is also the author of several books on the history
of Paris ("Les Cris de la ville"; "Zola photographe") and
on graphic design theory, aesthetics and interaction
with other arts: "L'ABC du Métier", Imprimerie
Nationale.
"La Mise en pages", Hoëbeke. "De la variation",
Le Promeneur. "Style et écriture", Albin Michel.
As a *diarist...* His "Continuo" and "Journal en désordre"
were published by Robert Laffont.
As a *music fan...* His love of music led him to
collaborate on various musical programs broadcast by
France Musique.
As an *illustrator...* He brought out a book of collages
inspired by the writings of Prévert, Hoëbeke
As a *photographer...* He created a book documenting
the outsider artist "Picassiette" (Raymond Isidore).
Massin also writes under the pen name Claude Menuet.
His impressive and wide-ranging cultural contributions
have earned him acclaim and distinctions in highly
varied circles.

Dank

Dieses Buch wurde von der aktiven, freundschaftlichen und diskreten Anteilnahme von Ralph Schraivogel begleitet. Zu unserer Freude war er so für die Zeit des Projekts ein «Mitarbeiter» der Plakatsammlung des Museum für Gestaltung Zürich, für die er schon seit Jahren Treue und Sympathie bekundet. Massin hat auf unvergleichliche Weise das expressive Potential der Typografie ausgelotet und war seit seiner ersten Begegnung mit Schraivogel 2003 dazu prädestiniert, einen Essay über seinen Kollegen beizusteuern. Bei beiden bedanken wir uns sehr herzlich für die Zusammenarbeit.

Thanks

Ralph Schraivogel has offered this book his active, friendly and discreet commitment. To our delight, this made him a "co-worker" for the duration of the project in the Zurich Museum für Gestaltung's poster collection, which he has supported faithfully and sympathetically for years now. Massin has plumbed the expressive potential of typography incomparably. Ever since his first encounter with Schraivogel in 2003 he was predestined to contribute an essay about his colleague. We would like to thank both of them most cordially for their co-operation.

«Poster Collection»

Herausgegeben von / Published by
Felix Studinka
Kurator der Plakatsammlung
Curator of the Poster Collection
Museum für Gestaltung Zürich
In Zusammenarbeit mit / in cooperation with
Bettina Richter, Wissenschaftliche Mitarbeiterin /
Scientific collaborator
Christina Reble, Publikationen / Publications
Museum für Gestaltung Zürich

Ralph Schraivogel

Konzept, Redaktion / Concept, Editing:
Felix Studinka, Christina Reble
Lektorat / Sub-editing: Mark Welzel
Übersetzung / Translation: Margie Mounier,
Ina Schüssler, Michael Robinson
Gestaltung / Design:
Integral Lars Müller / Hendrik Schwantes
Assistenz / Assistance: Gisèle Schindler
Lithografie / Repro: Ast & Jakob AG, Köniz
Druck / Printing: Vetsch + Co AG, Köniz
Einband / Binding: Buchbinderei Burkhardt AG,
Mönchaltorf

© 2003
Hochschule für Gestaltung und Kunst Zürich,
Zürcher Fachhochschule & Lars Müller Publishers

Museum für Gestaltung Zürich
Plakatsammlung / Poster Collection
Limmatstrasse 57
CH-8005 Zürich / Switzerland
e-mail: plakat.sammlung@museum-gestaltung.ch
http://www.museum-gestaltung.ch

Lars Müller Publishers
CH–5401 Baden / Switzerland
e-mail: books@lars-muller.ch
http://www.lars-muller-publishers.com

ISBN 3-03778-016-9
Erste Auflage / First Edition 2003

Printed in Switzerland